My Science Library

Changing Matter:
Understanding Physical and Chemical Changes

by Tracy Nelson Maurer

Science Content Editor:
Shirley Duke

Educational Media

rourkeeducationalmedia.com

Science Content Editor: Shirley Duke holds a bachelor's degree in biology and a master's degree in education from Austin College in Sherman, Texas. She taught science in Texas at all levels for twenty-five years before starting to write for children. Her science books include *You Can't Wear These Genes, Infections, Infestations, and Diseases, Enterprise STEM, Forces and Motion at Work, Environmental Disasters,* and *Gases.* She continues writing science books and also works as a science content editor.

www.rourkeeducationalmedia.com

Photo credits: Cover © YuriyZhuravov, PinkBlue; Pages 2/3 © CAN BALCIOGLU; Pages 4/5 © gresei, RicoK, Taras Kolomiyets, Zadiraka Evgenii, Algol; Pages 6/7 © Viktor88, Shebeko, BW Folsom, Africa Studio; Pages 8/9 © CAN BALCIOGLU, Smit, hans.slegers, Ljupco Smokovski; Pages 10/11 © davidundderriese, Nadezhda Bolotina, Blue Door Education; Pages 12/13 © Nadezhda Bolotina, Julian Rovagnati, Jiri Hera, Givoronskaya_Yana, jordache;; Pages 14/15 © Dmitry Naumov, Anna Baburkina; Pages 16/17 © Mikael Goransson; Pages 18/19 © HadK, Kurhan; Pages 20/21 © Arvind Balaraman, Alicar

The author thanks materials science engineer Michael Sullivan for his generous assistance and the entire Blue Door team.

Editor: Kelli Hicks

My Science Library series produced by Blue Door Publishing, Florida for Rourke Educational Media.

Library of Congress PCN Data

Maurer, Tracy Nelson.
Changing Matter: Understanding Physical and Chemical Changes / Tracy Nelson Maurer.
p. cm. -- (My Science Library)
ISBN 978-1-61810-107-5 (Hard cover) (alk. paper)
ISBN 978-1-61810-240-9 (Soft cover)
Library of Congress Control Number: 2012930305

Rourke Educational Media
Printed in the United States of America,
North Mankato, Minnesota

Also Available as:

rourkeeducationalmedia.com

customerservice@rourkeeducationalmedia.com
PO Box 643328 Vero Beach, Florida 32964

Table of Contents

Two Ways to Change

Everything is **matter**. It's made of something and takes up space. Matter changes in two ways: physical changes and chemical changes. Let's look at the differences!

Physical changes create different states, or forms, of the same matter. Water is still water if it changes from a liquid state into ice, a solid state.

Chemical changes create entirely new substances. After the chemical change, physical methods, such as cutting, drying, filtering, spinning, or changing temperature or pressure, can't undo the change.

Fire chemically changes wood into a new substance, ash or soot and gas. You can't bring the wood back after it has burned.

Spellbinding Alchemy

Ancient scholars, called **alchemists**, believed they could change metals into gold or produce other amazing results. Modern science has never proven their claims. However, their quests have inspired many stories, including *Harry Potter and the Sorcerer's Stone.*

Physical Changes

All matter is made of tiny moving particles called **molecules**. They move slower or faster in different states, such as solids, liquids, or gases.

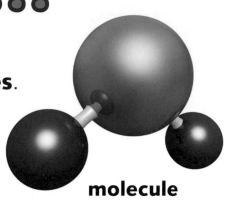

molecule

solid

liquid

A solid has a shape because its packed molecules move slowly.

A liquid takes the shape of its container. Liquid molecules have room to flow under and over each other.

A gas completely fills the shape of its container. Its fast-moving molecules have a lot of space between them and bounce off the container's walls. Gas molecules in air fill all of the space inside balloons.

gas

Physical properties help identify a substance and how it changes. When does it boil or melt? Is it magnetic? Does it **dissolve** with water?

Density is a physical property that describes how packed, or concentrated, a substance is. A crumpled paper ball has less density than a rock of the same size.

If the substance crushes easily, like a paper ball, it has low density. If it resists crushing, like a rock, it has high density.

Viscosity is a physical property that refers to how easily a liquid flows.

If the liquid is runny, like water, that's low viscosity. If it's gooey, like honey, that's high viscosity.

The Law of Conservation of Mass

Matter keeps its **mass,** the amount of itself, even after a physical change. For example, the steam's mass equals the mass from the original liquid's mass.

Chemical Changes

Chemical changes happen everywhere. In a chemical change, tiny atoms inside different materials' molecules rearrange and share their structures. This new molecular **bond** forms an entirely new substance, which is called a **compound**.

Did You Know?

Photosynthesis is a chemical change. The green **chlorophyll** in plants uses the Sun's energy to make food, called sugars, from water and **carbon dioxide**.

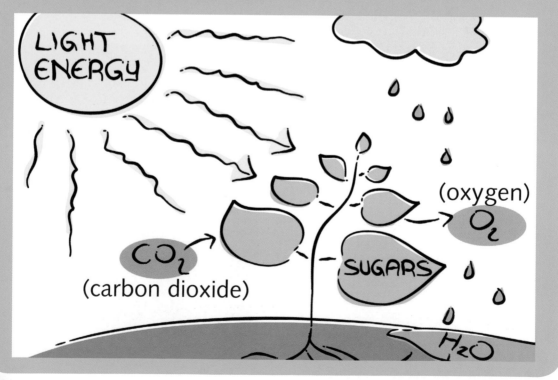

LIGHT ENERGY

(oxygen)

O_2

CO_2
(carbon dioxide)

SUGARS

H_2O

Carbon dioxide forms a compound when one atom of carbon and two atoms of oxygen combine.

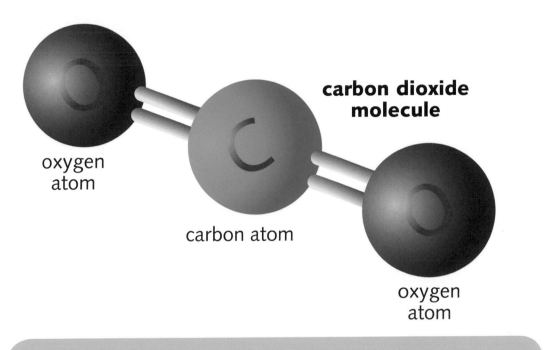

carbon dioxide molecule

oxygen atom

carbon atom

oxygen atom

Atoms

In each atom, the protons carry a positive charge and the electrons carry a negative charge. The number of particles in an atom makes the atomic weight. Millions of atoms could fit in this period.

electron   nucleus   electron

neutron   proton

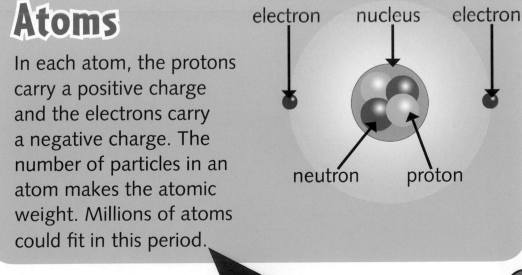

Some atoms easily make new compounds. These reactive atoms, such as hydrogen and oxygen, have charged particles that look for others to bond with to create an electrical balance.

Some atoms bond in other ways, too. Bonding allows atoms to balance their charges or fill spaces in their outer shells. They combine to form a very important molecule on Earth, called water.

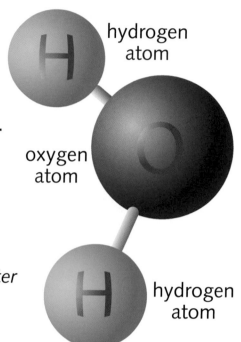

hydrogen atom

oxygen atom

hydrogen atom

Have you ever heard someone call water H_2O? H_2O is the chemical name for water. It means two hydrogen atoms and one oxygen atom.

Compounds In Your Kitchen

Table Salt = Sodium + Chlorine

Sugar = Carbon + Hydrogen + Oxygen

Baking Soda = Sodium + Hydrogen + Oxygen + Carbon

Neon, the noble gas used to make bright lights, is nonreactive. Neon atoms have the maximum number of electrons they can hold in their outer shell. Because missing electrons in the outer shell is what makes elements reactive, neon can't combine easily with other atoms.

Not all atoms invite chemical change. Gases such as neon, helium, and argon have stable electrical charges and do not usually make chemical compounds. They are called the noble gases.

The potential for an atom to change into a new chemical is an important property for researchers to know before they experiment. Oxygen changes easily and can produce fast results—maybe even an explosion!

Nothing burns without oxygen. But some materials, such as hydrogen, diesel fuel, or lithium metal, mixed with pure oxygen and heat burn so fast that they appear to explode.

Some chemical changes happen where you can plainly see them. A campfire leaves ashes behind, for example. Other chemical changes seem invisible, such as digestion inside your body.

Some chemical changes happen quickly. Vinegar and baking soda mixes into an explosion of bubbly carbon dioxide. Other chemical changes happen much more slowly. How they change depends a lot on the chemicals involved.

This chemical reaction made by combining vinegar and baking soda is actually two reactions happening very close together. The acid in vinegar reacts with the baking soda to form an unstable, mild acid. This acid breaks down right away into carbon dioxide and water. The bubbles come from the escaping carbon dioxide gas. The carbon dioxide is heavier than air so it flows over the jar.

Changing Fact

Chemical changes can occur slowly over time. Oxidation, or rusting, changes hard iron into crumbly dust when the oxygen in the air combines with the metal.

Molecules at Work

Wallace Hume Carothers, an American chemist, experimented with long chains of molecules called polymers in the 1930s. His work led to nylon. In 1940, shoppers bought more than 60 million pairs of nylon stockings. Since then, countless products have used nylon, from toothbrushes to military parachutes.

Your backpack is most likely made of nylon. What else will you use today made of nylon?

Today, researchers use the scientific method to find new ways of combining matter and its molecules.

Scientists ask questions and compare their answers to what's already known. They share their results. Other scientists test the ideas following the same steps.

The Scientific Method

1. Ask a question.
2. Conduct background research.
3. Form a new idea to test.
4. Test the idea with an experiment that can be repeated by others.
5. Draw a conclusion.
6. Report the results.

If an idea doesn't work out, start again at step 3!

Good or Bad Chemical Changes?

In the past three hundred years or so, scientists have created medicine, clothing, food, building products, and many other useful materials. But creating chemical changes can also bring pollution, poison, and other destructive results.

Acid rain looks like clean rain but it can kill fish, stunt tree growth, and spark asthma attacks.

Factories that burn coal, for example, release chemicals that react with water, oxygen, and other gases high in the atmosphere that make acid rain.

With more research, scientists will continue to learn more about changing matter. As they learn more, they will find new ways to help us and our planet.

Show What You Know

1. What type of change is happening when your car burns fuel? Why?

2. Can you think of other chemical changes you see every day?

3. If you could invent a new product, what would it be? How would it benefit humans?

Glossary

alchemists (AHL-kuh-mists): ancient scholars who studied mixtures as they tried to make gold and brew elixirs for everlasting life

bond (BAHND): the connection that joins two atoms or molecules to create a compound

carbon dioxide (KAHR-buhn dye-OK-side): a colorless gas produced by plants, exhaled by humans, and released by some burning materials and other chemical reactions

chlorophyll (KLOR-uh-fil): the green matter in plants that supports photosynthesis to make food

compound (KOM-pound): a combination of two or more particles, such as atoms or molecules

density (DEN-sit-ee): the quality or property of how compact a substance is in relation to its volume

dissolve (di-ZAHLV): to seem to disappear into another substance

mass (MASS): the measure of stuff, the something, of a substance

matter (MAT-ur): anything that has mass and takes up space

molecules (MOL-uh-kyoolz): the smallest bit of a substance that retains all the characteristics of the substance; a combination of atoms or atoms and other molecules

physical properties (FIZ-uh-kuhl PROP-ur-teez): qualities or traits something has

viscosity (VIZ-kahs-uh-tee): the quality or property of how a substance, especially a liquid, resists flow

Index

Websites to Visit

www.alchemylab.com/history_of_alchemy.htm

www.tpt.org/newtons/TeacherGuides_chemistryFood.php

www.chem4kids.com

About the Author

Tracy Nelson Maurer likes science experiments, especially the cooking kind! She lives in Minnesota with her husband and two children. She holds an MFA in Writing for Children and Young Adults from Hamline University.

Meet The Author!
www.meetREMauthors.com